Star and the Maestro

Star and the Maestro

How a Musical Bird Made Melodies with Mozart

by **Thor Hanson**

illustrated by **Matt Schu**

GREENWILLOW BOOKS

An Imprint of HarperCollinsPublishers

A long time ago in Vienna,

When pedigreed pets were a passion,

The purchase of creatures with fantastic features,
Was proof you were privy to fashion.

Star was a starling for sale in a shop,
Purveying fine pets in all shapes,
From peacocks to parrots,
Flamingos and ferrets,
Aardvarks, iguanas, and apes.

In a crowd of such uncommon animals,
Poor Star felt uncommonly plain,
He'd come from a farm in the country,
Where they'd called him a pest in the grain.

He wasn't exotic or flashy,

His fanciest feathers looked black,

With a faint purple sheen,

And maybe some green,

And a few simple spots on his back.

So when shoppers came calling he kept to his cage,

And watched all the other pets preen,

Convinced he'd grow old long before he was sold,

Unwanted, unloved, and unseen.

But while those finely plumed,

Might well have assumed,

That they would be everyone's choice,

Star had a skill that spilled from his bill,

In the form of a marvelous voice.

Few customers knew what a starling could do,
With the sounds that entered his ear,
Patching together peculiar songs,
From whatever he happened to hear.

When Star met a monkey
he hooted and whooped,

When he listened to kittens he purred,

He parroted piglets,
And mimicked macaws,

And neighed like a horse in a herd.

His bark was convincingly canine,
He credibly croaked like a toad,

And he fooled the whole store,
When he creaked like a door,
Or rattled like carts in the road.

But the song Star liked to sing most,

Was a haunting and musical phrase,

He'd heard someone hum it,

Or a street minstrel strum it,

And he'd sung nothing else for days.

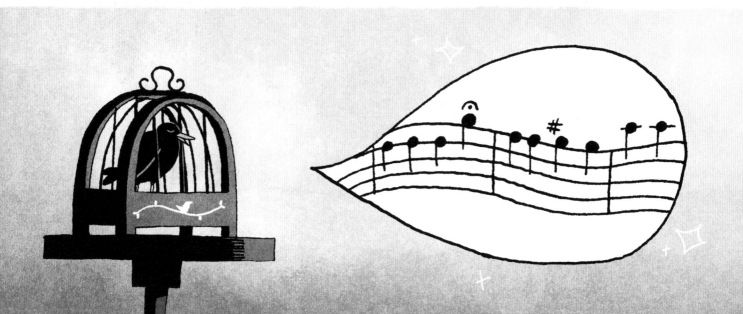

Those seventeen notes would alter Star's fate,
When a passerby stopped and was smitten,
Not believing he'd heard,
From the beak of a bird,
A song *he himself* had written!

"Das war schön!"* cried the maestro,
And raced to the shop,
Where he paid for the bird on the spot,

Tierhandlung

Thrilled to have found,

A companion in sound,

To whom a fine tune could be taught.

* "That was beautiful!"

And Star was glad too,
To meet someone who knew,
That a pet could do more than look pretty,

So he sang while he perched,

As his cage swayed and lurched,

While they walked through the heart of the city.

When they came to the maestro's apartments,
In a suite with a view of the street,

Star looked in and knew,

Like a dream coming true,

That his search for a home was complete.

The maestro kept instruments everywhere,
From flutes and violas to bass.
For a mimicking bird,
It was almost absurd,
To find so many sounds in one place!

Recitals and lessons and symphonic sessions,

Continued from morning to night,

Quartets and sopranos,

With harps and pianos,

Made Star sing aloud with delight.

But he also had fun when the concerts were done,
And he got to fly free from his cage,
While the maestro sat whistling and humming,
And writing things down on a page.

Outstretching his wings,

And plucking on strings,

Star tuned up his timing and tone,

Then echoed the notes that the maestro composed,

And added a few of his own.

The friendship of Star and the maestro,

Was born in this musical way,

And for people who know how to listen,

It still can be heard to this day.

The maestro in question was Mozart,

Whose music lives on as high art,

And sometimes contains,

A few special refrains,

From the starling who captured his heart.

MORE ABOUT MOZART & STARLINGS

The **common starling** is one of the best mimics in the bird world. Starlings can learn and repeat a huge variety of sounds, even human speech, and can memorize complicated patterns after hearing them just once. Native to Europe, common starlings were brought to North America in the nineteenth century and are now one of the most numerous birds on the continent.

Wolfgang Amadeus Mozart wrote his first piece of music at the age of five, toured Europe as a child performer, and died when he was only thirty-four. Widely recognized as a genius, he remains one of the most popular classical composers of all time. In the spring of 1784, Mozart purchased a starling that could sing a tune from one of his piano concertos. He referred to the bird by its German name, *Vogel Staar*, which historians have often shortened to Star. Star lived with Mozart and his family for three years, and when Star died Mozart was so distraught he held a formal funeral in the bird's honor. A few days later, Mozart finished a composition that many people found strange—it featured a hodgepodge of musical styles and melodies, just like the patched-together song of a starling.

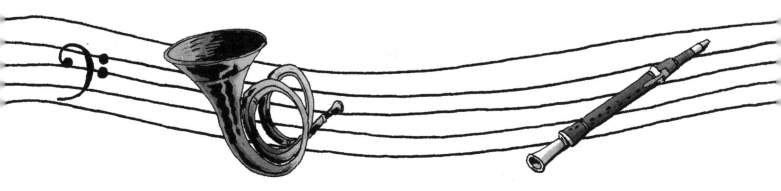

Did You Know?

When pedigreed pets were a passion . . . As European empires and world trade expanded, exotic pets became a status symbol for the upper classes. Wombats, mongooses, parakeets, monkeys—the stranger the better! Common local animals and birds like starlings weren't great status symbols, so for Mozart to purchase one meant that he thought Star's singing was very special.

His fanciest feathers looked black, With a faint purple sheen . . . In spring, the season when Mozart bought Star, starlings are mostly black with a purple and greenish tint. In the winter they are even plainer looking: brown with white spots. Why do birds have different colors at different times of the year?

Few customers knew what a starling could do, With the sounds that entered his ear . . . Male starlings patch together long songs in spring and summer to help them attract mates. Females can mimic sounds, too, but they are usually quiet during the mating season, when they are busy building nests, sitting on eggs, and raising chicks. Why are birds quiet on nests?

While the maestro sat whistling and humming . . . Mozart was famous for whistling and humming to himself all day, not just when he was composing. Some people think that Star might have learned to sing Mozart's piano concerto by overhearing the maestro hum it himself as he passed by in the street!

Acknowledgments

I am indebted to Lyanda Lynn Haupt and her wonderful book for adults, *Mozart's Starling*, and to a family of wild starlings that once nested in the crawl space above my bedroom.

For Erin, a herder of birds—T. H.

For Iris—M. S.

Star and the Maestro: How a Musical Bird Made Melodies with Mozart
Text copyright © 2024 by Thor Hanson. Illustrations copyright © 2024 by Matt Schu
All rights reserved. Manufactured in Italy. For information address HarperCollins Children's Books,
a division of HarperCollins Publishers, 195 Broadway, New York, NY 10007.
harpercollinschildrens.com

The full-color art was created digitally using Adobe Photoshop and Procreate® for iPad.
The text type is Carre Noir Pro.

Library of Congress Cataloging-in-Publication Data

Names: Hanson, Thor, author. | Schu, Matt, illustrator.
Title: Star and the maestro : how a musical bird made melodies with Mozart / by Thor Hanson ;
illustrated by Matt Schu.
Description: First edition. | New York : Greenwillow Books, an Imprint of HarperCollins Publishers, 2024. |
Audience: Ages 4-8 | Audience: Grades 2-3 | Summary: "The true story of the famous composer's pet
starling, who Mozart discovered when he walked past a shop and heard one of his own compositions being
sung by a bird"— Provided by publisher.
Identifiers: LCCN 2024006610 | ISBN 9780062676498 (hardcover)
Subjects: LCSH: Mozart, Wolfgang Amadeus, 1756-1791—Juvenile literature. | Composers—Austria—
Biography—Juvenile literature. | Starlings as pets—Juvenile literature.
Classification: LCC ML3930.M9 H36 2024 | DDC 780.92 [B]—dc23/eng/20240221
LC record available at https://lccn.loc.gov/2024006610

24 25 26 27 28 RTLO 10 9 8 7 6 5 4 3 2 1   First Edition
Greenwillow Books